THE CLEAR AND PRESENT TRUTH OF
DANIEL

THE SELF-INTERPRETING PARAPHRASE

Rapid Movements Publishing
Hampton, GA 30228

Copyright © 2021 by Tory St.Cyr

Printed in the United States of America
All Rights Reserved

Published by Rapid Movements Publishing
Hampton, GA 30228

Other books by Tory St.Cyr may be purchased at www.clearandpresenttruth.com

The author assumes full responsibility for the accuracy of all facts and quotations, as cited in this book.

ISBN: 978-1-7366073-6-7

Pictures and Illustrations

Babylonian Captivity By derivative work: Steerpike (talk)Arc_de_Triumph_copy.jpg: user: בית השלום - Arc_de_Triumph_copy.jpg, CC BY 3.0, https://commons.wikimedia.org/w/index.php?curid=4303855

By After Briton Rivière - Manchester City Art Gallery [sic!], Public Domain, https://commons.wikimedia.org/w/index.php?curid=50214

These digitally adjusted compilations of them the copyright of FreeBibleimages. Artist Jim Padgett. They are made available for free download under a Creative Commons Attribution-ShareAlike 3.0 Unported license.

By Unknown author - http://www.plinia.net/wonders/gardens/hgpix1.html, Public Domain, https://commons.wikimedia.org/w/index.php?curid=65909

https://www.cgtrader.com/

Freepik.com

Fiverr.com (pro_design_up)

This book is dedicated to Jack Blanco. Had it not been for your paraphrase, The Clear Word, I may have never had the courage to write this book.

Contents

Preface 9
Daniel 1 The Babylonian Captivity 11
Daniel 2 The Image of the Past, Present, and Future 15
Daniel 3 The Fiery Trial of the Three Hebrews 25
Daniel 4 The Humbling of King Nebuchadnezzar 31
Daniel 5 The Handwriting on the Wall 39
Daniel 6 Daniel in the Lion's Den 47
Daniel 7 The Animalistic Attributes of the Four Kingdoms 55
Daniel 8 The Cleansing of the Sanctuary 65
Daniel 9 The Seventy-Weeks Prophecy 73
Daniel 10 Daniel's Final Vision 79
Daniel 11 The Final War 83
Daniel 12 Three Prophetic Periods 97

Preface

What is a paraphrase? In the purest sense of the word, paraphrasing is to express the meaning of something written or spoken using different words to achieve greater clarity.

That being said, this Daniel paraphrase was created for the sole purpose of expressing what I believe the Book of Daniel reveals. In this, I hope you will gain further clarity on the meaning of the visions and dreams recorded by the prophet.

In case you are unfamiliar with paraphrases, you should understand that this book is not a Bible translation like the KJV or NIV. The contents of this book represent my understanding of Daniel's visions, dreams, and experiences, which are presented in the same chapter-and-verse format that the Bible utilizes.

Though this paraphrase should not take the place of the words written in authorized Bible translations, this paraphrase is an attempt to complement the Scriptures by providing you a verse-by-verse easy reader that makes the Scriptures as plain as possible.

This book is also a self-interpreter, meaning that the definition of the prophetic symbols and phrases are already incorporated into the verses. For example, instead of just using "beast" to describe a prophetic symbol representing a nation, I will go an extra step and provide the name of the kingdom that the beast represents.

The inspiration for this paraphrase comes from a complete Bible paraphrase called *The Clear Word* by Jack Blanco. While our writing styles differ in regard to the level of detail provided, *The Clear Word* was one of the reasons I decided to write this book, and it was always at arm's length of me during the writing process. And one day, I hope someone like you will decide to write a book on Daniel...and I can only hope that The Clear and Present Truth of Daniel will be at your arm's length.

(Please be aware that this paraphrase is also available as a component of a four-part parallel I wrote titled "The Daniel Parallel.")

Daniel 1

The Babylonian Captivity

THE CLEAR AND PRESENT TRUTH OF DANIEL

1. In Jehoiakim's third year as ruler of Judah, King Nebuchadnezzar, who, at that time was the Prince of Babylon, comes to Jerusalem with an army and surrounds the city.
2. Unfortunately for Jehoiakim, the Lord chooses not to intervene on his behalf, and Nebuchadnezzar takes the most valuable temple vessels back to Babylon for use in the service of his god Marduk.
3. Next, Nebuchadnezzar orders Ashpenaz, one of his officers, to take hostages from Judah's royal house and Judah's first families.
4. They are youths who are handsome, intelligent, have a good understanding of various subjects, and can learn Aramaic literature and language.
5. These hostages are given royal treatment from Nebuchadnezzar. This treatment means that they will receive their meals directly from the king's table, which includes everything he eats. His master plan is to provide training and a menu for three years and then examine them to see if they are fit to serve.
6. Among the hostages taken from the royal house of Judah are Daniel Hananiah, Mishael, and Azariah.
7. Daniel Hananiah, Mishael, and Azariah pass the examination and are selected to serve in the king's court. The young men are then castrated and assigned new names by Ashpenaz, who is in charge of all eunuchs. Accordingly, Daniel's name is changed to Belteshazzar; Hananiah is now called Shadrach,

Mishael will be called Meshach, and Azariah will be known as Abed-nego.
8. Daniel decides he will not dishonor God by consuming the king's food and drinks that have been offered to idols. Therefore, the Hebrew asks for permission to abstain from any food or drinks that would defile him.
9. God had brought Daniel into favor and compassion with Ashpenaz
10. However, after the prince of the eunuchs hears Daniel's request, he says, "I am scared because the king has provided specific food and drinks for you guys, and once he notices how anemic you'll look, compared to all the others, he will hold me responsible."
11. Daniel then pays a visit to Melzar, the personal tutor to the three Hebrew boys, and says to him,
12. "Put us to the test for ten days; give us only vegetables to eat and water to drink.
13. Then compare our appearance against those who are eating the king's food, and then make a decision according to the results."
14. Melzar listens intently to Daniel and agrees to this ten-day test.
15. At the end of ten days, it's apparent that Daniel and the three Hebrew boys are healthier than all the others who were eating the king's food.

16. So Melzar allows them to stay on this diet and eliminates the king's food so that they will no longer be forced to eat from his table.
17. So God blesses Daniel and the three Hebrew boys with wisdom and skill in practically everything they did. To Daniel, God not only blesses him with wisdom and skill, but he also blesses Daniel with the ability to interpret visions and dreams.
18. At the end of their three-year training, Ashpenaz takes Daniel and the three Hebrew boys to be examined by Nebuchadnezzar.
19. As the king examines them, he soon discovers that Daniel, Hananiah, Mishael, and Azariah are far more advanced than all the others. So the king decides to make all four of them permanent members of his court.
20. Soon Nebuchadnezzar will discover that, regardless of the issue or problem, Daniel and his friends are far more superior in solving them than any magician or psychic in Babylon.
21. Daniel continues to serve in the royal court, even after Babylon is conquered by Cyrus.

Daniel 2

The Image of the Past, Present, and Future

THE CLEAR AND PRESENT TRUTH OF DANIEL

1. Two years after Nebuchadnezzar's inaugural year, Nebuchadnezzar has a dream that really troubles him. As a matter of fact, this dream troubles him so much that he can no longer sleep.
2. So he calls all his established fortune tellers, astrologers, scientists, and priests and asks them to explain to him his dream.
3. He says to them, "I had a dream last night that really bothered me, and I need you guys to tell me what my dream meant."
4. The Chaldeans respond to Nebuchadnezzar in his native tongue and say, "May the gods give long days and everlasting years to the king, my Lord. Describe your dream to us, and we will tell you its meaning."
5. Nebuchadnezzar replies, "I can't remember what my dream was about, but I know that I had a dream, so listen, and listen good. If you guys can't tell me what my dream was and give me the meaning of my dream, I will slice each and every one of you limb from limb and turn your homes into public waste dumps.
6. On the other hand, if you can tell me what I dreamed and give me the explanation of the dream, I will provide you with gifts and rewards, so tell me my dream and its meaning now!"
7. "Your Majesty," they reply, "if you would just tell us what you dreamed, we know we can provide you the meaning of that dream."

DANIEL 2 • THE IMAGE OF THE PAST, PRESENT, AND FUTURE

8. Nebuchadnezzar responds, "I clearly see that you guys are stalling for time. You think because I can't remember my dream, I'll eventually forget about this whole situation.
9. Well, listen closely; if you don't tell me what I dreamed, there is only one outcome for you because I know what you guys are trying to do. You'll try to make something up, hoping that by the time you tell me, I would've forgotten the dream. So tell me what I dreamed, and if you can tell me this, then I'll know that you can tell me the meaning as well."
10. The men try to reason with the king, "Your Majesty, no one can do this; and no man of power or authority that demands such a thing from his priests, fortune-tellers, and astrologers.
11. Please understand this is extremely difficult, and the only way that your dream can be known is if the supreme gods in heaven reveal it, but those gods don't talk to men."
12. At this point, Nebuchadnezzar goes into a rage and orders the execution of every wise man in Babylon.
13. So the orders are drawn up that every wise man is to be executed, and officers arrive to carry this out on Daniel and his friends.
14. Arioch, commander of the king's guard, finds Daniel and confronts him with the king's order; however, Daniel responds in wisdom and tact.
15. Once Daniel understands the king's order, he asks

Arioch, "Why would a harsh order like this come from the king so urgently?" Then Arioch explains the whole story to Daniel.

16. After understanding the situation, Daniel requests permission to stand before the king to ask for a 24-hour extension. Daniel promises that by tomorrow he will know the dream and will be able to give him the interpretation as well.
17. King Nebuchadnezzar listens to Daniel's proposal and agrees to its terms. Daniel quickly goes home and shares everything with Hananiah, Mishael, and Azariah.
18. Daniel tells them that they must pray for mercy from the God of heaven to show them the dream and the interpretation so they are not executed with the other wise men of Babylon.
19. That night, God reveals to Daniel the exact dream He had previously given to Nebuchadnezzar. Daniel, filled with joy and thanksgiving, praises the God of heaven.
20. As he's praising God, Daniel says, "Praise God forever and ever! All wisdom and power are His!
21. Times and Seasons are not regulated by happenstance or coincidence; it is God who controls these things. It is He who removes kings and sets up kings. He is the One who gives wisdom to those we call wise and knowledge to those we call intelligent!
22. It is He who reveals mysteries that no one else has

DANIEL 2 • THE IMAGE OF THE PAST, PRESENT, AND FUTURE

the capability to know. He knows what's in the darkness because the light shines from Him.

23. I thank You and praise You, Oh God of my fathers! I thank You and praise Your holy name because what we asked, You have revealed to me. You have blessed us to know the king's dream!"
24. Immediately, Daniel goes to see Arioch, who is also in charge of carrying out the king's orders to execute Babylon's wise men. Daniel says to Arioch, "You won't have to execute the wise men of Babylon. Take me to the king, I know what he dreamed, and I can also tell him what it means."
25. Arioch rushes Daniel to the king and says to the king, "Your Majesty, I have found someone among the Jewish captives who claims he can tell the king his dream and interpret it for him."
26. "Daniel," begins Nebuchadnezzar, "Do you think you can tell me my dream and what it means?"
27. "Your Majesty," Daniel responds, "I just want to say that there is no philosopher, astrologer, or fortune-teller living on this planet that can do what you're asking.
28. However, there is a God in heaven who can reveal and explain all mysteries. As a matter of fact, it was this same God who gave you this dream in order for you to know what will happen in the future. So let me tell you the dream you had while you were sleeping:
29. Now, before you went to sleep that night, you were

sitting on the edge of your bed, wondering what will happen to your kingdom in the future; And the God of heaven actually revealed it to you!
30. I know this, not because I'm more intelligent than everyone, but God revealed your same dream to me to save the lives of your advisors and because He wanted you to know what will happen to your kingdom.
31. In your dream, you saw an enormous statue of a man. The statue seemed to be glowing with light all around it, and it was very frightening to see.
32. The head of this statue was made of pure gold, its chest and arms were made of silver, its waist and hips were made of bronze.
33. Its legs were made of iron, and its feet were made partly of iron and partly of molded clay.
34. Now, while you were observing this statue, a huge boulder broke off a mountain without anyone touching it; this boulder was propelled with great force towards this statue striking its feet of iron and clay, and the impact caused the feet to immediately crumble into pieces.
35. When the feet crumbled, the rest of the statue collapsed and broke into fine particles similar to the particles of grain left over when they are separated from the plant. Then a strong wind came and blew the dust away, and there was no trace of the metals left over. And finally, you watched the boulder get

DANIEL 2 • THE IMAGE OF THE PAST, PRESENT, AND FUTURE

bigger and bigger until it became a mountain that filled the whole earth.

36. That is what you saw in your dream, and here is what it all means:

37. You are the greatest king among earthly kings. It is the God of heaven that has given you this Kingdom of Babylon, and has given you power, might, and glory,

38. Not only that, but He has given you rulership over people, animals, and birds; so the golden head on that statue represents you and your kingdom.

39. But after some time passes, the Medes and Persians will conquer Babylon. Now even though they will conquer this kingdom, Medo-Persia will be inferior to Babylon in glory and moral values, just as silver is inferior to gold. Then that kingdom will be replaced by Greece, which is represented by bronze, but that kingdom will be even more inferior in glory and moral values than the Medes and Persians—while at the same time ruling a larger part of the world.

40. Then Rome will come into power. This kingdom will be as strong as iron. And just as iron can crush all other metals, Rome will crush every kingdom that stands in its way. However, this kingdom will be even more inferior in glory and moral values than all the kingdoms that preceded it.

41. And as you saw the feet and toes that were partly clay and partly iron, you must understand that in the last days, the continuation of iron Rome, known as Protestant America, and the ten Kings of the East, will be allied with the Papacy. In this manner, the Roman iron and Papal clay will be joined together.

42. And as the toes on the feet were partly iron and partly clay, the union that the kings of this world will establish with Protestant America and the Papacy will be partly strong and partly fragile.

43. Just as you saw the iron mixed with clay, Protestant America will attempt to bind this worldwide union together with Papal ideology. However, just as clay won't stick to iron, neither will this union hold together.

44. These nations will continue their quest to create a worldwide union right up until the time God comes and sets up the Kingdom of Christ. This Kingdom's reign will be established when Christ is seen coming in the clouds, which will bring an end to all other earthly kingdoms. Christ's Kingdom will never be conquered; it will stand forever.

45. And just as clear as you saw the stone, untouched, break loose from the mountain and shatter the iron, brass, clay, silver, and gold into pieces, you can be assured that everything you saw will happen because the dream is accurate and you can be confident in its interpretation."

46. Then Nebuchadnezzar falls on the ground and bows before Daniel out of sheer appreciation for him. He

also orders incense and sacrifices to be made on Daniel's behalf.

47. The king then says to Daniel, "It is undeniable that your God is the greatest of all the gods because you were able to tell me what my dream was and the interpretation of it!"

48. Then the king lavishes Daniel with gifts and promotes him to be the ruler over the whole province of Babylon. He was also placed in authority over all the king's advisers.

49. Daniel then requests Shadrach, Meshach, and Abednego to be his assistants. Thus, his three friends become helpers with the affairs of the province, while Daniel takes care of the affairs of the city, working closely with the king.

THE CLEAR AND PRESENT TRUTH OF DANIEL

Daniel 3

The Fiery Trial of the Three Hebrews

1. After a while, Nebuchadnezzar decides to build a statue similar to what he saw in his dream. However, in an effort to challenge the prophecy and show that Babylon will last forever, he makes the whole statue out of gold! The image, which stands about 88 ft tall (including the platform) and 9 ft wide, is placed in the plains of Dura within the Babylonian territory.
2. Then Nebuchadnezzar orders all his officials to participate in the dedication of this image. This dedication includes princes, governors, commissioners, judges, treasurers, advisers, sheriffs, along with anyone else in an official position of authority. He summons all of them to this dedication ceremony.
3. All the princes, governors, commissioners, judges, treasurers, advisers, sheriffs, and other government officials arrive. They all stand before this image that Nebuchadnezzar set up.
4. Then Nebuchadnezzar's official announcer yells with a loud voice, "People of all nations, there is a command for you:
5. When you hear the sound of the horns, followed by the flutes, the various harps, bagpipes, and all other musical sounds, you are commanded to fall on your knees, bow to the ground, and worship this golden statue that King Nebuchadnezzar has set up.
6. Now, anyone who does not kneel down and worship will be executed on the spot by burning to death in a

DANIEL 3 • THE FIERY TRIAL OF THE THREE HEBREWS

heated furnace."

7. Then the horns, flutes, and harps begin playing, and immediately the people fall down and begin worshipping Nebuchadnezzar's golden image.
8. While this is taking place, some of the Chaldeans watch the Hebrews hoping they'll be able to accuse them of being disloyal citizens.
9. These same Chaldeans find their way to the king and say, "May Your Majesty live forever!
10. You commanded us that at the first sound of the horns, flutes, harps with other stringed instruments, bagpipes, and all the other musical sounds, everyone present should fall on their knees and bow in worship before your golden statue,
11. And that decree also states that anyone who didn't obey that command would immediately be executed by being thrown into the heated furnace.
12. Well, the three Jews you put in charge over the province of Babylon, Shadrach, Meshach, and Abednego, have disrespected you. Not only do they disregard our gods, but they even have the nerve to refuse to worship this image you have set up!!"
13. Nebuchadnezzar goes into a rage. He then orders his guards to bring Shadrach, Meshach, and Abednego to him at once.
14. The guards bring the three Hebrews to the king, and he says to them, "Is it true, Shadrach, Meshach, and Abednego, that you are refusing to bow down and

worship the golden statue that I have erected?"

15. He continues, "Listen very closely. I'm going to give you one more chance to demonstrate your loyalty to Babylon. Once the music begins playing and I see you bow down and worship the image, then all is forgiven; however, if you don't bow down and worship, I will burn all three of you alive inside of the furnace. Now, I don't know a god that can deliver you out of my hands...do you know of one?"

16. Shadrach, Meshach, and Abednego answer the king, "Your Majesty, it is not even necessary for us to defend ourselves in this matter because we have already made a decision.

17. You asked, do we know a god that can deliver us out of the fiery furnace. Well, the answer is yes. Our God, the One whom we worship, can deliver us from the burning furnace.

18. However, even if He chooses not to save us, one thing is guaranteed; we will not bow down and worship this golden image."

19. At this point, Nebuchadnezzar goes into a furious rage! His face becomes red with anger as he looks at Shadrach, Meshach, and Abednego. He then orders his men to make the furnace temperature seven times hotter than usual.

20. Once the furnace is hot enough, Nebuchadnezzar, in order to ensure nothing supernatural can intervene, commands some of his strongest men to tie up

DANIEL 3 • THE FIERY TRIAL OF THE THREE HEBREWS

Shadrach, Meshach, and Abednego.

21. These strongmen tie up the three Hebrews with full head-to-toe attire, including their robes, head coverings, and all other clothing; then, the strong men throw the three Hebrews into the blazing furnace.
22. The furnace is so hot that the strong men's clothes catch fire and burn them alive in the process of throwing the Hebrews into the furnace.
23. Shadrach, Meshach, and Abednego fall into the burning furnace while they are still tied up.
24. All of a sudden, Nebuchadnezzar jumps to his feet in total shock. He then turns to his advisers and says, "Correct me if I'm wrong, but didn't we throw three men into the furnace?" The advisers reply, "Yes, your Majesty, there were three men."
25. Nebuchadnezzar points to the burning furnace and cries out, "Look! Now there are four men...and they are all walking around inside the burning furnace unharmed!" Then Nebuchadnezzar looks a little closer at the furnace, and he says, "And the fourth one looks like the One they told me would come....the Son of God!"
26. Then the king walks as close to the door of the furnace as possible, and he calls out to the three Hebrews, "Shadrach, Meshach, Abednego, servants of the Most High God, get out of the furnace and come here." Then they all stand there and watch as

Shadrach, Meshach, and Abednego walk right out of the furnace.

27. As the Hebrews walk out of the furnace, everyone crowds around to examine them. Not only is their skin free of burns and blisters, but their hair shows no evidence of being in the fire, and they don't even smell like smoke!

28. Then Nebuchadnezzar shouts, "Praise to the God of Shadrach, Meshach, and Abednego who sent His Angel to deliver them out of my hands. They trusted in Him, and their loyalty is why they disobeyed my orders and risked their lives, rather than bowing and worshipping a deity that's not their God.

29. Therefore, I'm going to make the following law: Regardless of where you are born or what language you speak, if anyone says anything remotely disrespectful about the God of Shadrach, Meshach, and Abednego, he will be ripped in pieces, limb from limb and his house will be made a public place for human waste. The reason for this law is because no other god can deliver people the way their God delivered them."

30. Then the king promotes Shadrach, Meshach, and Abednego, making them even greater throughout Babylon.

Daniel 4

The Humbling of King Nebuchadnezzar

1. Nebuchadnezzar sends this message to all nations and language groups in his kingdom and nations he had conquered: Peace to all of you.
2. I want to testify of all the great miracles and wonderful things that the God of heaven has done for me.
3. What a great and wonderful God He is! His miracles are nothing short of incredible! His kingdom is the only kingdom that will last throughout the ceaseless ages of eternity.
4. Here's my testimony: A little over seven years ago, I, Nebuchadnezzar, was relaxing in my palace thinking about all my accomplishments and was feeling quite good about myself.
5. I dozed off and had a dream which turned into a nightmare. I was very frightened by the dream, and on top of that, I couldn't get the terrible images out of my head.
6. So, once again, I called all the wise men of Babylon to stand in my presence in order to get the interpretation of my dream.
7. And, once again, they could not interpret my dream, even after I was able to tell them what happened in the dream!
8. Finally, I called Daniel, whom I named Belteshazzar after my god because I know the gods' spirit is with him. He arrived in my presence, and I told him my dream. Here is what I told him:

9. "Chief of the governors over all the wise men of Babylon, I know that the spirit of the holy gods is with you, and they keep nothing hidden from you. I have had another dream. I want you to listen to what I have seen and tell me its meaning.
10. I fell asleep in my palace, and while I was sleeping, I dreamed that I saw a huge tree standing in the middle of the earth. This tree was the biggest tree that I had ever seen in my life.
11. As I watched, the tree grew bigger, and it seemed that the top of the tree reached all the way to outer space. As a matter of fact, it was so tall that everyone on the earth could see this tree.
12. The leaves were beautiful, and there was a lot of fruit...so much fruit that it could feed everyone! This tree provided shade for the animals of the field and a home for all the birds of the air. Everyone received their nourishment from this tree.
13. I dreamed all of this while lying in bed, but then a holy angel from heaven came down and visited me.
14. Then, with a loud voice, this angel said, 'Chop this tree down, trim its leaves, and scatter its fruit. Drive away the animals receiving its shade and shoo away the birds living in its branches.
15. But make sure you leave the stump and the roots. Place iron and bronze bands around the stump to preserve it and leave the grass around it as he will share the same habitat as the animals in the wild.

16. His ability to reason like a human will be taken from him, and in return, he will become deranged and wild like an animal. He will remain in this condition for the next seven years.
17. This was all decided by the heavenly assembly of watchers so that the world will know that The Most High is the ultimate ruler of this earth, and it is He that allows men to become king, even the lowest of humanity if He so chooses.'
18. So, Daniel, this was the dream that I had. Now, please tell me what all this means because all the wise men in Babylon are clueless; but I know from our experiences together that you have power from the holy gods, and they will tell you what all this means."
19. Then there's an awkward silence. Daniel knows the meaning of the dream but is stunned when he realizes the magnitude of its fulfillment. King Nebuchadnezzar, sensing Daniel's hesitation, breaks the silence and says, "Belteshazzar, I can tell by your hesitation that the dream is bad news for me." Daniel remains quiet. Nebuchadnezzar continues, "but I can take it; don't let it bother you... just tell me what it means." Then Daniel, while looking into the eyes of the king, says, "My Lord, I sure wish this dream applied to your enemies and those that are against you!
20. However, the tree that you saw grow strong and tall...so tall that anyone who looked at the sky could

see it;

21. Which had beautiful leaves and was bearing many fruits for everyone, under which the animals of the field came to rest and where the birds built their nests;
22. Well, my Lord," Daniel continues, "that tree represents you. You see, just like that tree, you have become great and strong. And just like that tree, you can be seen by everyone, and your dominion spreads throughout the world.
23. My Lord, then you saw an angel, which said, 'Cut down the tree and destroy it but leave the stump and the roots. Put a band of iron and bronze around it and let it get wet with the morning dew like the grass of the field. Whoever represents this tree will live with the animals for seven years.'"
24. Daniel looks directly at the king and says, "So that's what your dream meant. The Most High God has decreed this to happen to you, my Lord.
25. Your mind will leave you, resulting in your being driven away from society. You will begin to think like an animal, and you will dwell with animals in the fields. You'll do everything like them; you'll eat like them, you'll sleep like them, you'll live like them. All of this will take place for the next seven years until you learn that God is the true Ruler of this world's Empires, and whoever He chooses, that individual will rule the known world.

26. However, your kingdom will be restored back to you, which is why the stump and the roots remained. However, this will only happen after you acknowledge God's supremacy.
27. Now, if I may advise you, my Lord, please show your repentance by doing right; show mercy to the oppressed, and perhaps the Lord will shorten your punishment."
28. Unfortunately, the king doesn't listen to Daniel, and events happen to him, just as Daniel prophesied.
29. About one year later, King Nebuchadnezzar is taking a walk on the roof of his palace.
30. As he's walking and observing the breathtaking views, he suddenly stops; his eyes pan over the whole city, and he fills up with pride exclaiming to himself, "This is the great Babylon! And I am the one who built it!! This is the most glorious kingdom that has ever existed, and it was because of my intelligence! It was because of my might and power and superiority!"
31. As soon as he makes this statement, he hears a voice saying, "King Nebuchadnezzar, your kingdom has just been taken from you.
32. You will lose your mind and be driven from society to live with the animals of the field. For the next seven years, you will eat grass like an ox until you learn that the Most High God rules in the affairs of men and can give your kingdom to whomever he wants."
33. Immediately, Nebuchadnezzar begins losing his

mind. Once his advisors realize what's happening, they take him to the fields, where he begins eating grass just like an ox. His body becomes wet with the morning dew, his hair becomes matted and unruly, and his fingernails grow like bird's claws.

34. Then, after seven years, the king's mind suddenly comes back to him. Once he realizes his sanity is back, he stands in the open field, looks up to heaven, and begins praising God, saying, "I praise and worship the One who lives forever! Only His reign lasts forever; only His kingdom endures from generation to generation!

35. Everyone else is irrelevant! It doesn't matter if it's heaven or earth; His sovereignty is everywhere! Who is powerful enough to stop Him? Who is wise enough to question Him?"

36. Once King Nebuchadnezzar's closest advisers get word that their king's mind is back, they, with open arms, get him out of the fields in order to restore him to his rightful place on the throne. Everyone is so happy to have him back, and it becomes apparent that he is viewed even more honorably than before the ordeal.

37. Nebuchadnezzar comes to one conclusion after all this takes place. He proclaims, "I, Nebuchadnezzar, praise and honor the God of heaven, and I glorify the King of kings, whose ways are right and just toward everyone but who also humbles those who are lifted

up by pride and power."

Daniel 5

The Handwriting on the Wall

THE CLEAR AND PRESENT TRUTH OF DANIEL

1. It's now several years later. Nebuchadnezzar is dead, and his grandson, Belshazzar, is co-ruler with his father, King Nabonidus. On this particular day, King Belshazzar decides to throw a big party to which he invites one thousand of the most important people in Babylon. Princes, wealthy statesmen, and beautiful women are all there, drinking and dancing the night away.
2. It's at that moment an intoxicated Belshazzar gets an idea. He orders his guards to bring in the gold and silver cups that his grandfather, Nebuchadnezzar, took from the Temple in Jerusalem so that he and all his guests can drink from them.
3. The guards leave and come back shortly afterward and in their hands are the golden cups from the temple. They pour wine into the cups and start drinking. If that's not enough, while they are drinking, they begin to praise the gods of Babylon.
4. They continue to drink as they direct their praise towards the gods of gold, and of silver, of brass, of iron, of wood, and of stone.
5. Suddenly, a hand appears out of nowhere and begins writing on the plaster right above the candlestick. Everyone at the party stares in unbelief.
6. Belshazzar's face turns ghastly pale with terror, his knees begin to buckle, and he starts profusely shaking.
7. The hand disappears, but the words that it wrote

DANIEL 5 • THE HANDWRITTING ON THE WALL

remain imprinted on the wall. Belshazzar sees the words; however, he is not able to determine what they mean. The king then begins yelling for his astrologers, fortune-tellers, and priests...anyone that can tell him what this message means. Once they arrive, Belshazzar says to them, "If anyone here can read the writing on this wall and tell me what it means, I will dress you in royal purple, and put a gold chain around your neck, and you will be the third most powerful man in the whole kingdom after my father and me."

8. The rest of the wise men arrive and begin to examine the writing on the wall. However, none of them are able to make sense of the words written by the hand.

9. Once the king realizes that no one can read the message, it terrifies him even more to the point his face becomes pale like a dead man; this frightens everyone at the party.

10. The queen, who was made aware that something troubling was happening at the party, arrives at the banquet hall. After looking at the wall and seeing the terror on the face of Belshazzar and his guests, she turns to her son and says, "May Your Majesty live forever. There's no reason to be afraid or perplexed over this.

11. There's someone in Babylon in whom the spirit of the gods' live, and I'm confident he will be able to tell you what all of this means. When your grandfather was

king, this man was found to have insight, understanding, and wisdom of the gods. Your grandfather placed him in charge of all the astrologers, fortune-tellers, and priests.

12. Your grandfather did this because the spirit of the gods is in him. He has great insight and understanding; he can interpret dreams, solve riddles, and explain mysteries. His birth name is Daniel, but the king named him Belteshazzar. Summon him here, and he will be able to interpret the writing for you."

13. Belshazzar nods his head, and his guards bring Daniel before him. As Daniel stands in front of the king, Belshazzar says to him, "Are you the same Daniel that my grandfather Nebuchadnezzar brought to Babylon as a Jewish captive?" Daniel nods his head and responds, "Yes, I am."

14. Belshazzar continues, "I have heard that the spirit of the gods is in you, and you have great insight and understanding with the ability to interpret dreams, solve riddles, and explain mysteries."

15. Daniel attentively listens as Belshazzar points to the wall and says, "So, by now, I'm sure you've noticed that there are words written on that wall over there. I have no idea what they mean, which is the reason all my wise men, astrologers, and priests were brought in to read it, but unfortunately, they can't do it.

16. And that's why you're here, Daniel. I heard that you have the ability to interpret mysteries such as this. So

DANIEL 5 • THE HANDWRITTING ON THE WALL

here's what I'm going to do for you: If you can explain these words written on this wall over here, then I will place my royal purple on you, I'll put a chain around your neck, and you will be the third-highest ruler behind my father and me in the whole kingdom."

17. Daniel pauses for a moment, then responds to the king, "Your Majesty, I appreciate the offer, but I don't need any gifts for what I am about to tell you. I will read what it says, and then I will tell you what it means.
18. The Most High God made your grandfather, Nebuchadnezzar, the king. He also gave him majesty, glory, and great honor.
19. He was so great that people from all over the world feared him and trembled at his word. And Nebuchadnezzar did whatever he wanted to. He determined who lived and who died, or who was promoted or demoted…it was in his hands.
20. However, at some point, he became proud and arrogant, so he was removed from power.
21. He was driven from society. His mind was made like an animal. He ate grass like an ox and slept outside until he realized the Most High rules, and He alone appoints men as rulers over kingdoms.
22. King Belshazzar, you knew all of this, yet it didn't change your heart.
23. Instead, you showed no respect for God. You took the cups from his holy temple in Jerusalem so you and

your royal guests could drink from them while praising the gods of gold, silver, bronze, iron, wood, and stone. They aren't real, but the God of heaven, the One you mock, is the God who holds your very life and breath in his hands, and yet you totally insulted and disrespected him.

24. And this was the reason that God sent the hand that you saw writing on this wall.
25. So here is what it says: 'MENE, MENE, TEKEL, UPHARSIN.'
26. And this is what it means: MENE means that God has numbered the days of your kingdom, and they are coming to an end.
27. Tekel means that you have been examined by God, and the results of that examination are that you don't measure up to the standard that God has set for you.
28. Peres means that because you failed the examination, God is going to take this kingdom from you and divide it between the Medes and the Persians."
29. Then, as Belshazzar promised, he orders Daniel to be dressed in royal purple and a has gold chain placed around his neck. Daniel's name is then proclaimed amongst the nobles as the third highest ruler in the kingdom.
30. However, that very night, the city is taken as Daniel prophesied it would. The Medes and Persians divert the Euphrates River, walk right into the city, take the guards by surprise, and kill Belshazzar.

31. And Darius the Mede, at sixty-two years old, takes the throne as the new ruler of Babylon.

THE CLEAR AND PRESENT TRUTH OF DANIEL

Daniel 6

Daniel in the Lion's Den

1. After taking the Babylonian throne, Darius divides the country into one hundred and twenty provinces and appoints governors over each of those provinces.
2. He also appoints three more officials (Daniel being one of them) as overseers of the governors.
3. Once again, Daniel proved to be so much more excellent than any of Darius' government officials that Darius considers placing Daniel in charge of the whole kingdom!
4. Some of the officials within the government take notice of this, and jealousy begins to manifest itself among them. So they formulate a plan. They decide to find some fault with Daniel...some kind of negligence on his part, in order to take him down.

    However, after observing Daniel for some time, they begin to realize they can't find a single neglect on his part!
5. In desperation, the conspirators call a secret meeting. They knew that Darius would eventually put Daniel in charge of the whole kingdom if they didn't find something wrong with the Hebrew. So the conspirators come up with a devious plan: "Men," they begin, "If we can't find anything wrong with his work, then we will find something wrong with his religion!"
6. Everyone begins to smile because they know Daniel will be more loyal to his God than he will be to the king. And so they make their way to see Darius. They

enter his presence and greet him with the usual salutation, saying, "May Your Majesty live forever!"

7. One of the conspirators speaks up and says, "Your Majesty, as your presidents, governors, counselors, and officials, we believe everyone's loyalty should be tested." King Darius sits up in his chair. "We believe," he continues, "that everyone should be tested to see if they are loyal to you. If anyone fails this test, they don't deserve the privilege of your rulership, and that individual should be thrown into the lion's den.

8. To make this happen, all you need to do is sign this document, and this decree officially becomes part of the unchangeable Medo-Persian law."

9. Darius briefly looks at the document, then places his royal seal on it. The decree has officially been added to the law of the land.

10. Daniel, not long afterward, is informed of this new law. However, this doesn't change Daniel's routine. Knowing that what he is about to do is now considered breaking the law, Daniel still goes to his rooftop, opens his window, and prays toward Jerusalem as he has customarily done three times a day.

11. However, this time, he is being watched. The conspirators knew Daniel's routine, so they simply watched and waited for Daniel. Their plan paid off, and now they have the evidence they need to get rid of Daniel once and for all!

12. The men hastily make their way to the king. As they stand in front of Darius, they begin their rehearsed opening statement. "Your Majesty," they begin, "didn't you sign a decree that for thirty days no one can pray to any god or man except you? And if that decree is broken, that man or woman is to be thrown into the lion's den?" King Darius confidently responds to the inquiry, "Absolutely!" He continues, "And this is officially part of the Median and Persian law, so I can't even change it."
13. The conversation is going according to plan. The men then respond to the king, "Your Majesty, you know that captured Jew named Daniel? Well, he is ignoring the law and continues praying to his God."
14. Darius slowly sits back in his chair. He now realizes that this whole time, these men were simply out to get Daniel, and they used his power, his throne, and his name to do it. After the men left, King Darius spent all day trying to find a way to save Daniel.
15. Time has passed. The sun has set, and the men have now returned to remind Darius of their earlier conversation. "Your Majesty," they begin, "we just wanted to remind you, in case you forgot, that you can't change this law. There is nothing that you can do here."
16. Darius reluctantly gives in and sentences Daniel to death. As the guards bring Daniel to his place of punishment, King Darius and his princes meet him

DANIEL 6 • DANIEL IN THE LION'S DEN

there. The guards bring Daniel to King Darius as the king is desirous of having one last conversation with his friend. With tears in his eyes, he says to Daniel, "I have no choice but to carry out this sentence...and...I don't know what tomorrow holds, but what I do know is that you've been faithful in serving your God, and if He is what you say He is, then I truly believe that He will rescue you from these lions."

17. After this, they lower Daniel into the lions' den, roll a huge boulder over the entrance and put sealer all around the boulder. This is done so no one can break the seal and rescue Daniel or even kill him should the lions fail to do so.

18. King Darius returns to his palace, but he's so distraught that he can't eat his dinner and has no desire for his usual evening amusements. This is because all he can do is think about Daniel. The king goes to bed, but he can't sleep. So he stays up all night worrying about Daniel.

19. As soon as morning arrives, King Darius gets dressed and hurries to the lion's den to see if Daniel survived. He wonders if Daniel's God has been able to protect him.

20. As King Darius arrives at the last known spot he saw Daniel alive, he anxiously calls out, "Daniel! Servant of the Most High God! Has your God delivered you?"

21. For a moment, the king hears silence. Then a familiar voice is heard from the lions' den. "Your Majesty,"

Daniel begins, "may you live forever!
22. My God sent his angel and took away their desire to eat me so that they didn't even touch me! My God did this because he knew that I was innocent and that I have been loyal to you all this time."
23. King Darius, unable to hide his excitement at hearing Daniel's voice, quickly orders his guards to throw a rope to Daniel and pull him out of the lion's den. When he lifts up Daniel, everyone is shocked to see that there's not even a scratch on him! There is only one reason for this miracle: Daniel trusted in his God.
24. After this, King Darius orders those who conspired against Daniel to be thrown into the lion's den along with their wives and children. Unfortunately for them, Daniel's angel had already left, and the lion's appetites returned. This becomes painfully evident as the lions begin mauling and tearing them apart while they are being lowered into the den...even before their feet touch the ground!
25. After Daniel's enemies were all placed in the lion's den, the king makes the following announcement to everyone in his kingdom: "Peace to every one of you!
26. I am making a decree that throughout my kingdom, men and women should show respect for the God of Daniel. His God is the living God and will be so forever. His kingdom will never be destroyed, and His dominion will last forever."
27. I am a witness that He is able to save anyone He

wants, and He performs miracles in heaven and on earth. This is the God who took away the lion's appetites and saved Daniel, His servant."

28. Daniel gets restored to his position and faithfully serves Darius until the Median king's death. Afterward, Daniel serves King Cyrus and is just as prosperous under Cyrus as he was under Darius.

THE CLEAR AND PRESENT TRUTH OF DANIEL

Daniel 7

The Animalistic Attributes of the Four Kingdoms

1. Let's go back a few years and revisit the first year of Belshazzar's reign. At that time, God gave me visions and dreams, in which I kept a record of what was shown to me. Here are the important details of what God revealed:
2. One vision, in particular, happened at night. What I saw were peoples, multitudes, nations, and kingdoms from every direction of the known world being stirred up with the spirit of war. I also saw that there would be revolutions and conquests in order for these kingdoms to obtain more power.
3. Then the Lord showed me four animals representing four empires that would ultimately dominate the world through these wars of conquest. Not simultaneously, but one after another, they were to arise among the peoples, multitudes, nations, and kingdoms and have dominion over the known world. While these four world powers were all part of the same vision, they all had unique qualities that made them different from each other.
4. The first kingdom, presented as a lion, was Babylon. What makes Babylon unique is that, just as the lion is the king of the jungle, Babylon will be considered the most glorious out of all the kingdoms that follow it. And the manner it conquered and spread itself throughout the region was like no other as it overpowered the known world. However, God will only allow Babylon to rule for so long; eventually, He

is going to humble this nation, and its reign will be over.

5. Then I was shown the next world power to come up among the peoples, multitudes, nations, and kingdoms of the known world will be Medo-Persia. This nation was presented to me as a bear. And just as a bear is considered inferior to a lion, Medo-Persia will be less glorious than Babylon. Then I noticed that the bear was raised up on one side, which revealed that Persia would one day conquer Media. I also noticed the bear had three ribs in its mouth representing Egypt, Assyria, and Babylon—the three world powers it subdued. God will permit Medo-Persia to dominate all other nations.

6. After this, God showed me the next world empire that would rise to power would be the Greek Empire. God presented this kingdom to me as a leopard with four wings and four heads. God used wings to emphasize how quickly this empire will conquer the known world. It will achieve world dominion faster than all its predecessors, but eventually, this kingdom will end up being divided into four separate nations toward the north, south, east, and west, which is why the leopard was presented with four heads.

7. As these Greek nations declined from internal strife, I saw the fourth Beast that symbolizes the fourth world power. However, this time, the animal that God chose to represent this empire was unlike anything I had

ever seen! All I know was that this animal was extremely frightening! It was very strong, with great iron teeth, and it used those teeth to devour everything in its path. This was the animal that God chose to represent the last world power! God was letting us know that this nation will not only dominate the known world, but it will crush and devour any nation in its path. This Beast was very different from all the other Beasts in a number of ways. To begin with, this creature had ten horns which represented ten lines of kings.

8. While I was watching these horns that represented ten kingships, I saw another horn rise up among them, but this horn was significantly smaller than the others. I would later understand that this Little Horn represented all the kings of the Roman Empire, which will begin as a small city in Italy. This horn will later transition from symbolizing kings to symbolizing the Popes that will rule during the Empire's Papal phase. I then watched as the Little Horn destroyed three of the ten horns that had arisen. This was an indication that Rome's rise to dominance would only occur after it conquered the nations ruled by these three existing kingships. I also saw that these kings and Popes would never be satisfied and would continue seeking for more riches, power, and glory—even to the point of making blasphemous claims against God and His Church.

9. I continued watching till I saw thrones being set up, and The One, who precedes time, sat down. His robe was as white as snow, and His hair was white like wool. His throne and the wheels of His throne were literally on fire!
10. Then a stream of fire shot out from His throne. Thousands and thousands of angels attended to Him, and it looked like tens of thousands multiplied by tens of thousands of angels stood before Him, ready to serve Him. This was the beginning of the great and final judgment that was set to take place before the end of the world. The Books were opened, and the lives of men passed in review before God.
11. I continued watching as the vision transitioned to the close of the judgment, and I could hear the Little Horn blaspheming God with his words. I then witnessed the Beast that was controlled by the Little Horn being destroyed and his body being burned in hellfire. The Beast's destruction revealed the punishment given to those who followed the system set up by Rome.
12. By this time, Egypt, Assyria, Babylon, Medo-Persia, and Greece's period of dominance will have already passed, but their influence of false worship and hostility towards God's people will continue to live through Rome until God decides its season of dominance is finished.
13. I then saw another vision that night. It was as if God took me back to the start of the judgment that begins

in heaven. Jesus, the One who is often called The Son of Man, was surrounded by so many angels that He looked as if He was riding on a cloud. These angels brought the Son of God to the Most Holy Place within the heavenly sanctuary before The Father, The One who precedes time.

14. I then saw that once the judgment was finished, God would take back this world from Satan and give it to the rightful heir—His Son. He will be made ruler over all nations and every language so that people everywhere should serve Him. His authority will be an everlasting authority, and His sovereignty will never end.

15. Now once the vision ended, I was really bothered by what I had seen. I was troubled because I wasn't completely sure what God was trying to tell me.

16. Then I looked up and realized I was still in vision. I know this because I was still seeing the throne of God. So I decided to approach one of the angels present there, and I asked him what all of this meant. And this is what he told me:

17. "These are the four great world powers that will successively dominate the earth from your time until the end of the world.

18. However, those who give their hearts to the Lord will inherit the earth and become citizens of God's kingdom. This is the kingdom that will ultimately supersede all these other kingdoms and will last

forever."

19. I listened, but I just had to know more about this Roman Empire. The fact that its kingship will switch from kings to Popes made this power different from all the other powers. Also, knowing this kingdom will dominate the world by crushing every nation in its path really got my attention.

20. I wanted to know more about those ten kingships whose territories were absorbed into the Roman Empire. Likewise, I was curious to understand more about the three kingships that were destroyed by this empire. I also wanted to know how this nation continued to seek more power and how its Popes blasphemed against God. And last but not least, I really wanted to understand how this nation began so small and insignificant but quickly became so great and powerful.

21. Then, I saw that this same religious power, led by Popes and priests, will persecute the true believers of God, and no one will stand in its way!

22. It was then revealed to me that this war against the saints will continue until God the Father announces judgment in favor of His people and the time arrives for them to have dominion over the earth. I now realized why this judgment scene was so important!

23. Then the angel provided more details about Rome. He said to me, "As you've seen, the Kingdom of Rome will be the fourth kingdom in a series of world-ruling

empires. You also saw how Rome will crush all other nations in order to dominate the world.

24. The ten horns that you saw represent the kings of Egypt, Assyria, Babylon, Media, Persia, Greece, and the four kingdoms that will rule the divided Greek Empire. If you remember, those four Greek kingdoms were north, south, east, and west. Prior to Rome's dominance, Eastern Greece, which will be ruled by Seleucus, will conquer Northern Greece, which will be ruled by Lysimachus. This conflict will leave the divided Greek Empire with three horns instead of four. As Rome begins conquering the known world, it will subdue the remaining three kingships of the divided Greek Empire—the Macedonian Kings in the west, the Seleucid Kings in the east, and the Ptolemaic Kings in the south.

25. However, Rome won't stop there. Soon afterward, the Roman kingship will be overtaken by its religious leaders, known as Popes. As the continuation of the Roman kingship, these Popes will elevate themselves by making declarations and decrees and taking the prerogatives of God. Ultimately, they will be recognized in place of God. The Church that rules over this kingdom will also chain up Bibles, limit the common people from studying the sacred text, and encourage its priests to interpret scriptures for its citizens. And whoever disobeys this religious power's commands will end up being persecuted relentlessly.

If that's not enough, the Papacy will also make everyone believe that the Ten Commandments have been changed. They will elevate the first day of the week as the replacement for the seventh-day Sabbath, resulting in most of the Christian world believing the Sabbath has been abolished. However, some will refuse to follow the Papacy, and they will be persecuted by Rome for 1260 years, which will begin in 538 AD and end in 1798 AD.

26. But the Heavenly Courts will convene and come to a ruling that the Papacy's authority must be eliminated and its worldwide kingdom destroyed.
27. Then God's people will inherit the everlasting kingdom on the earth made new. They will be able to witness the fullness of its majesty, knowing it will last forever. It will also be governed by the Most High God, and everyone there will obey and serve Him from a loving heart."
28. After the angel's words, I came out of the vision, but to be honest with you, I was deeply troubled by what I had witnessed. So troubled that it began to affect my features, and I became pale like a dead man. However, I decided not to tell anyone what I had seen, so I kept it all to myself.

THE CLEAR AND PRESENT TRUTH OF DANIEL

Daniel 8

The Cleansing of the Sanctuary

THE CLEAR AND PRESENT TRUTH OF DANIEL

1. A couple of years later, I had another vision. This vision seemed to be related to the previous one, but I was given a little more detail this time.
2. This particular vision was given to me while I was on official business for the king at his other palace in Susa, which is in the province of Elam. It happened as I was taking a walk along the Ulai River.
3. In this vision, I saw a river. Standing next to that river was a ram with two horns representing the kings who co-ruled this nation. I realized one kingdom would have power over the other when I saw one of its horns was higher than the other, even though it arose last.
4. This nation, symbolized as a ram, will conquer westward, in the direction of Babylon, northward, in the direction of Assyria, and southward, in the direction of Egypt. No other nation will be able to withstand this kingdom or defend against it. This nation will do whatever it wants, and as a result, it will become powerful.
5. Now, while I was trying to process what I had just witnessed, a creature resembling a goat suddenly came upon the scene. This animal represented a nation that would rise to prominence in the west. This nation will conquer the known world faster than all its predecessors, which is why the goat never touched the ground in the vision. One other thing I noticed about the goat is he had a large horn between his eyes.

DANIEL 8 • THE CLEANSING OF THE SANCTUARY

6. I continued watching this goat moving towards the ram. Then as the goat got closer, it charged at the ram with a full head of steam.

7. I watched as the goat violently slammed into the ram, destroying him and both of his horns. The nation represented by the Ram was destroyed by the nation symbolized by the goat, and no other nation helped the ram.

8. The ruler of this nation is symbolized by the goat's large horn, which will continue to grow in strength and power. However, at the height of his power, he will be broken, and in his place, four lesser kings will begin consolidating territory towards the north, south, east, and west.

9. The kings of these four kingdoms will fight against each other until another nation rises in the west. Symbolized by a little horn, the kings who consecutively rule this nation will begin as a small insignificant kingship but will ultimately become the most powerful kings in the world. In their quest for world dominion, the kings who rule this nation will conquer the remaining territories of the east and the south. Centuries after these kings conquer the known world, they will attempt to conquer a new frontier—the glorious things of God.

10. As Church and State combine, these kings will become more religio-political. They will also become exceedingly powerful—especially against God's people, who will be considered as bright lights in the Kingdom of Heaven. Through deception, the little horn will not only cause the downfall of God's people, but this power will also annihilate them.

11. But the little horn won't stop there. These kings will then begin elevating themselves in an attempt to take the place of Christ, the Prince of heaven's people. These religious kings will do everything in their power to take away the continuation of Judaism called Christianity, and through deception and persecution, will employ measures designed to block God's people from their connection to God's heavenly sanctuary.

12. A vast amount of people within the Roman Empire will become believers in this false system of religion and will persecute those who are part of the continuation of Judaism called Christianity. All of this will happen because everyone will be deceived into breaking the law of God. As the centuries pass, the truth will be more suppressed and dragged down to the point that most of the world will believe the religion of these kings is the true universal religion of God.

13. While still in vision, I then heard two angels talking. One of them said to the other, "How long is the vision regarding the continuation of Judaism called Christianity, and the Pagan-Christian mixture known as Catholicism that brings ruin, and the assault

against the heavenly sanctuary and the host of believers that enter it by faith?"

14. Then that other angel turned to me as if I had asked the question and said, "After 2300 years, God will do what the Jewish High Priest does in the earthly sanctuary on The Day of Atonement—He will go into the Most Holy place in the heavenly sanctuary and purify it. This is where God opens the books of heaven, and the work of judgment begins. God will vindicate His Name and His people."

15. So that's what I saw in the vision, but I still didn't understand it. I tried to make sense of what I had just seen and what the angel told me, but I was still confused about what it all meant. Then, suddenly, another angel appeared in front of me; this one had human features about him.

16. Then I heard a voice say, "Gabriel, explain the vision to Daniel and help him understand it."

17. Then Gabriel came towards me. What a sight! His countenance beamed with the pure light of heaven. As he got closer, I could sense the awesome and glorious power of God Almighty, and I could tell that he came directly from the presence of God Himself! In fact, I was so overwhelmed with awe and reverence that it got to the point that my body began to tremble, and it felt like at any moment, I would be snuffed out of existence! At that point, all I could do was fall on my face. I then heard Gabriel talking to

me. "Daniel," he began, "though you may not understand everything you've seen, what you must understand is that the vision extends all the way to the time of the end of the world."

18. This whole conversation had taken place while I was still in vision, and even though I was awake, I must've been in some sort of trance. Then, Gabriel put his hand on me, lifted me off the ground, and placed me back up on my feet.

19. He continued and said, "I want to give you a little more detail around the wars, conquests, and persecution that takes place towards the end of time. However, God won't allow it to continue forever, and He has determined when all this ends.

20. As you already know, the ram that you saw with the two horns represents the joint empire of Media-Persia. However, what you don't know is that the two horns on the ram represent all the kings who rule Media and all the kings who rule Persia.

21. And what about the goat with the great horn? You already know the goat represents the kingdom of Greece, but what you haven't been told is that the great horn between his eyes represents Greece's first king, Alexander the Great.

22. In the prime of his power, Alexander will suddenly die. This untimely death will send his top generals and closest officials into a frenzy as they attempt to obtain power and territory for themselves. Ultimately, this

will cause Greece to fragment into four smaller kingdoms. And though these four kingships will rule the same territory as Alexander the Great, they will never be as great as the Greek King.

23. Centuries later, apostasy will become prevalent. And just when it seems it can't get any worse, another power will rise to conquer the world. This nation will be known as the Roman Empire. Its kings will be brutal and ferocious, and they will speak in a language totally unfamiliar to the children of Israel. This is the nation that will rise to rule the known world.

24. The Roman kingship will become mighty and powerful. They will utilize this power to cause extraordinary destruction to those who oppose them. These kings will prosper in doing everything they can to destroy God's mighty and holy Church.

25. Once the Roman Kingship converts from Paganism to Christianity, they will enact policies for the Church. These policies will spread very quickly at the hands of these kings, who will magnify themselves as having heavenly insight in order to blend Pagan lies with Christian truth. Not only will these kings be responsible for destroying many without a sword, but they will also elevate themselves against Jesus Christ! However, never forget that in the end, this power will be destroyed—not by the hand of humans, but by the Hand of God.

26. The part of the vision you saw regarding the 2,300 hundred years is guaranteed to happen. However, don't stress yourself out by trying to understand everything you saw because this part of the vision is sealed, and it will be several centuries before it will be revealed."
27. Then I came out of the vision. However, I was so overwhelmed by what I had seen, that for days afterward, I felt sick. Then, I finally went back to work carrying on the king's business, but I was still in awe of what I had seen in the vision and desperately wanted to know what it all meant; however, I just couldn't grasp it.

Daniel 9

The Seventy-Weeks Prophecy

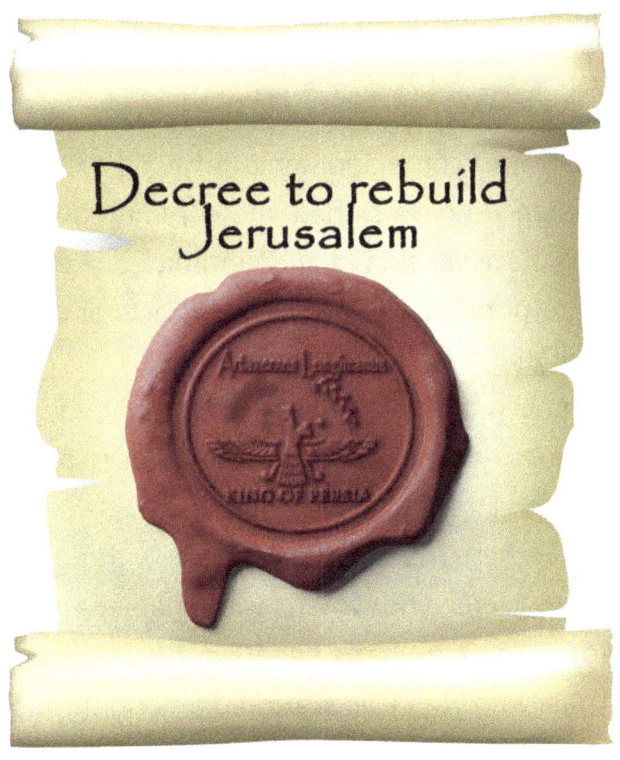

1. Darius, the son of Ahasuerus of the Medes, was made king over the realm of Babylon.
2. In the first year of his reign, the Lord revealed to me through the book of Jeremiah that Jerusalem would be in ruins for seventy years, and that time period was coming to an end soon.
3. Once I understood this, I began pleading with the Lord in prayer. I also began fasting with sackcloth and ashes.
4. I prayed to the Lord my God, and I confessed my sin and the sins of my people. And this is what I said to Him: "Lord, you are great and awesome. You, who keeps the covenant with those who love you and keep your commandments.
5. Father, we have sinned and committed iniquity. Not only have we sinned and committed iniquity, but we have done disgustingly wicked acts and have done everything contrary to your will.
6. We even ignored your prophets that you sent to us to speak to our kings, princes, leaders, and even our whole nation.
7. Oh Father! You are synonymous with righteousness, and we are synonymous with shame. And that goes for all of us, even the people of Judah, Jerusalem, and Israel who you have scattered among throughout the countries because of the sin they committed against you.
8. All of us have sinned. This includes our kings, our

princes, and our leaders. We are all guilty because we have sinned against you.

9. And even though we've done all this against you, you are still merciful and forgiving.
10. Lord, we are supposed to be your people, but yet we have disobeyed you and have refused to follow your laws given to us through your prophets.
11. Yes, all of us have broken your law. We have turned our backs on you, so we can't see you, and have covered our ears so we can't hear your voice. And this is why all the curses written by Moses are being poured on us. All of this is happening because we have sinned against you.
12. All this has shown us that your Word is true. You warned us of the consequences, yet because of our disobedience, Jerusalem has been ravished more than any other city in the world.
13. Moses told us what would happen, but we didn't care. We kept sinning against you and refused to pray for deliverance from our wicked desires in order to understand your will.
14. Lord, I know you patiently waited. However, I also know you eventually had to discipline us. But Lord, even in punishment, you are righteous.
15. You are the same God who rescued us and brought us out of Egypt. This rescue wasn't a small event, but you did it with a great display of power that made a lasting impression even to this day. But even after all

of that, we still find ourselves sinning against you.
16. Father, you've always done what is right. Please don't let Jerusalem continue to be punished for our sins and the unrepentant wickedness of our ancestors. Even the heathens are calling us a disgrace!
17. So we humbly ask that you hear this prayer and that you please look favorably on Jerusalem and your temple. However, not for our sake but, Lord, for your sake.
18. Please hear my prayer, oh Lord. Incline your ear. Don't close your eyes toward me but see how your city is in ruins even now. Father, we know we don't deserve anything, but we also know that you are merciful.
19. Father, please hear me! Please forgive us! Do not delay our deliverance! We believe in your promises. Lord, Jerusalem is your city, and we are your people."
20. Now, right while I was in the middle of praying and confessing my sins and Israel's sins
21. Gabriel, the same angel I had seen earlier, showed up again. This was around the time of the evening offering.
22. "Daniel," he said, "I have come back to give you a better understanding and more insight regarding the vision.
23. As soon as you began praying, God gave me a command to help you, so I am here because you are precious to God. Now listen closely to what I am about to say so that you can better understand the

DANIEL 9 • THE SEVENTY-WEEKS PROPHECY

vision previously given to you.

24. Out of the 2,300 years previously mentioned, you must understand that 490 of those years have been allotted to your people and Jerusalem. Those 490 probationary years are given to your people and Jerusalem in order for them to stop intentionally choosing to disobey God, to turn away from their sins, to be reconciled back to God, to accept God's grace, receive His righteousness which never fades, to preserve the integrity of the vision by living up to its fulfillment, and to sanctify the Lord by recognizing his holiness and authority over them.

25. Now, it's important that you hear this, but it's also important for you to understand that in the near future, there will be three decrees to restore Jerusalem. The decree that will be of most interest to you and the people of Israel will be the decree that commands the rebuilding of Jerusalem along with the restoration of its religious ministration and civil government. This command, given by King Artaxerxes, will be carried out in 457 BC and is significant because 49 years later, Jerusalem will be completely rebuilt, and 434 years after this restoration, Jesus Christ will emerge as the promised Messiah. By that time, the court in front of the temple will be recreated along with the walls so it will once again be a fortified city. Unfortunately, this restoration will happen during troublesome times as the Persians will attempt to eradicate your people.

26. And though the Son of God will emerge 434 years after Jerusalem's restoration, He will be crucified not long afterward. While no fault will be found in the Messiah to warrant this death, those who refuse to accept Him will be slaughtered by the Roman armies, who will also destroy Jerusalem and the sanctuary. Sadly, destruction and war will continue happening until the very end.

27. During the last seven of the 490 years allocated to the Jews, Jesus the Messiah will put all His effort into saving the lost sheep of Israel. He will do this by teaching and preaching a new covenant. However, after three and a half years, Jesus will be crucified. His crucifixion will put an end to the earthly sanctuary services and the Levitical laws that point to His death. This will leave Israel with three and a half years remaining until their probation is closed. Unfortunately, your people will continue to reject God's grace and mercy and will continue to do things that God considers an abomination. This will ultimately be the reason behind Jerusalem's destruction by the Roman armies. However, just as surely as Jerusalem will be destroyed, Rome will eventually meet a similar fate."

Daniel 10

Daniel's Final Vision

1. Daniel, who was also known as Belteshazzar, received one final revelation from God. This revelation was given to me in the third year of Cyrus, the King of Persia. This message was made clear to him, but there was a great struggle in order to understand.
2. This was revealed to me after I fasted and cried out to the Lord in prayer for three full weeks.
3. During this period, I ate no delicacies, no meat, or any rich foods. I did not drink any wine and even denied myself personal luxuries, such as fragrant oils, until the three weeks were over.
4. On the twenty fourth day of the first month, I took a walk by the great Tigris River.
5. Suddenly I received a vision, and I saw Someone standing in the distance dressed in a white linen robe with a belt made of Ophir gold around His waist.
6. His whole body seemed to radiate with light, and His face was so bright it looked like a flash of lightning. His eyes appeared like a blazing fire, His arms were the color of highly polished brass, and His voice sounded like a large multitude of people speaking in unison. This was the Son of God!
7. I was the only one who saw Him, but those who were with me felt His presence, which was so powerful that they all ended up running away!
8. Despite being all alone, the vision continued, and I had no strength left in me.
9. However, I could still hear Him speaking. As He spoke

to me, I was lying on the ground like I was in a deep sleep.
10. Then a hand touched me and helped me get up on my hands and knees, which by this time, were both trembling.
11. It was Gabriel, the angel. He reassured me by saying, "Daniel, you are highly esteemed by God, so I need you to stand in place and listen carefully to what I'm about to tell you." At this point, I stood to my feet, but they were trembling.
12. He continued, "Don't be afraid, Daniel. At the moment you started fasting and praying for understanding, your voice was heard, and that's why I'm here with you now.
13. The reason for the delay is that Cyrus, the Prince of the Persian Kingdom, fell under the influence of demonic powers and refused to cooperate with God's plan for your people. However, Michael, the One who was a Prince from the beginning, showed up and helped me. He also remained there with the Prince of Persia to keep those demonic forces in check.
14. Now, I'll explain what will happen to your people in the coming days, which will extend to the end of the world."
15. While he was talking, I had a hard time keeping my head up. Eventually, my head slumped toward the ground, and I couldn't open my mouth to speak.
16. Then Gabriel, who had veiled his brightness in order

to look like a man, came and touched my lips. At that point, I was able to speak again and said unto him, "I feel overwhelmed because I am so weak and powerless right now.

17. How can I ask you about what I've been shown when I can't even talk? Not only am I weak, but I'm even having a hard time breathing."
18. At that point, he touched me again, and I felt my strength returning.
19. Then he said, "Don't be afraid. You are highly precious in the eyes of God. Peace be to your soul and strength to your body." Then I responded to him and said, "Okay, now I'm strong enough to listen, please continue."
20. Then he said, "Do you know, the only reason I came here was to ensure that you understood the vision? Now that you understand, I will return and continue working on the Prince of Persia; however, soon afterward, my attention will be on the coming Prince of Greece.
21. But first, let me show you what is written in the record of truth. Then, I will return, as I am the only individual who has been given the special assignment of ensuring that you receive this truth besides Michael, your Prince."

Daniel 11

The Final War

1. Gabriel continued, "Which is also one of the reasons God sent me to strengthen and protect Darius during the first year of his rulership.
2. With certainty, here are the events that will happen in the future:
After King Cyrus is gone, three more kings will consecutively rise to power and rule the empire. Finally, a fourth ruler, named King Ahasuerus, will rise after them. However, Ahasuerus will have more wealth than any of them. He will use that wealth to build one of the world's largest armies and stir up all the Greek city-states to unify against the Persian Empire.
3. But a mighty king named Alexander the Great will rise to power in Greece. He will defeat Persia's last king, Darius III, and absorb his territory. Then, as the ruler of the former Persian Empire and unified Greek city-states, Alexander the Great will rule the known world, and no one will stop him.
4. However, at the height of his power, Alexander the Great will die suddenly. This untimely death will cause a frenzy among his generals and top officials, who will ultimately split the kingdom northward, eastward, southward, and westward. Alexander's son will also be assassinated before he can succeed his father, and the kingdom will be fractured into multiple territories. The Greek Empire will never be united as it was under Alexander the Great because all his top officials will

tear the kingdom into multiple pieces, but only four of those pieces will be relevant.

5. One of Alexander's former generals, Ptolemy I Soter, will become very powerful and rule Egypt as the King of the South. Later, a Babylonian governor named Seleucus I Nicator will arrive in Egypt seeking asylum. He will serve Ptolemy as a general, and Ptolemy will help Seleucus conquer Babylon and much of the eastern territory. This conquest will make Seleucus the King of the East, and he will become more powerful than Ptolemy. Later, Seleucus will defeat Lysimachus, the King of the North, in the Battle of Corupedium, making Seleucus the King of the North and East. Seleucus will be the greatest of Alexander's former generals and will rule the largest territory.

6. Conflicts will ensue between the northern and the southern territories, eventually leading to a peace treaty. To honor the treaty, Antiochus II, the then King of the North, will divorce his wife Laodice and marry Berenice, the daughter of Ptolemy II, the then King of the South. However, Laodice will end up poisoning her estranged husband, Antiochus, then murdering Berenice and her child.

7. Berenice's brother, Ptolemy III, who will at that time be King of the South, will hear of his sister's death and will raise an army to avenge her. During the Third Syrian War, he will attack Syria and be victorious against the then King of the North, Seleucus II.

8. Ptolemy III will also recover the sacred idols previously taken by the Persians. These, along with silver and gold, will all be taken back to Egypt. And though Ptolemy will be very successful, this will be the last time he will attack Seleucus II.
9. After some time, Seleucus II will recover from his previous defeat and will raise an army against Ptolemy III to regain the lost idols that were taken. However, Ptolemy will once again defeat Seleucus, sending him back to his home in the north empty-handed.
10. Seleucus II will return to discover that his father's other son, Antiochus Hierax, has assumed control of Asia Minor. In order to take the throne from Seleucus, Antiochus will assemble an alliance of hostile nations and destroy Seleucus' army in the War of the Brothers. But, after his victory, Antiochus will learn that his alliance provoked a conflict back home, and he will be forced to wage war in his own territory.
11. Years later, the King of the South, Ptolemy IV, will lose territory to Antiochus III due to an act of betrayal. This betrayal will enrage Ptolemy and drive him to go on the offensive to attack Antiochus, the King of the North. These massive armies will clash in the Battle of Raphia, resulting in Antiochus' defeat.
12. After the war, Ptolemy IV will be so caught up in his success that he will miss the opportunity to wipe out his enemy for good. Even though Ptolemy will have

destroyed thousands of Antiochus' men, his failure to pursue Antiochus will allow the northern king to rebuild his army. Ptolemy's failure will make his victory a temporary one.

13. Years later, Antiochus III will return to invade and occupy Ptolemaic territories. However, the Ptolemaic commander will recapture these provinces, and Antiochus III will respond by assembling an even larger army than the one that previously fought at Rafah. Not only will he come back to the south with a larger army, but he will also have more battle equipment.

14. During that time, the King of the South, Ptolemy V, will not only receive threats from Antiochus III, he will also receive threats from the ancestors of those who've historically oppressed Israel. In an attempt to overthrow their colonizers, fierce Egyptian insurgents will bring violence and bloodshed to the region during the Great Egyptian Revolt. These insurgents will rise with the hopes of ending Ptolemaic control over Egypt, but their insurrection will fail.

15. Years later, Antiochus Epiphanes will rise as the King of the North. He will nearly conquer all of Egypt as the Ptolemaic armies won't be able to stand up to him. Even God's Chosen people will be unable to defend themselves against him, and he will force them into false worship and persecute them.

16. Unfortunately for Antiochus Epiphanes, the rise of the

Roman Republic will stop him from fully conquering Egypt. The Romans will eventually come against the Seleucid Empire and defeat it. Rome will do as it pleases, and no one will be able to stop it. This nation will not only conquer the land of Israel, but it will also destroy Jerusalem and scatter its inhabitants.

17. Rome will focus on conquering the known world, including the children of Israel. During that time, Julius Caesar, a powerful Roman Consul, will be at war with another Roman Consul named Pompey Magnus. In pursuit of Pompey, Julius will go down to Egypt, where he will become involved with a daughter of the Cleopatrian family line—Cleopatra VII. Her father will place her under Roman guardianship which will lead to Caesar appointing her as the Queen of Egypt. However, power will corrupt her, leading her to kill her brother. Soon after, her life will end in tragedy. And even though she develops relationships with two Roman consuls, her loyalties will always remain with Egypt.

18. After this, Julius Caesar will turn his attention to the Iberian Peninsula to destroy the remaining opposition forces led by Pompey's two sons. Once the opposition forces of Pompey are destroyed, Julius will believe he has put an end to all remaining opposition against him; but the war against Pompey will ultimately be the catalyst for Julius' downfall. His close friend Decimus Brutus will conspire with the

Roman Senate to have Julius Caesar killed.

19. After Julius Caesar crushes his opposition, he will return to Rome, where he'll be elected dictator for life. However, the Roman Senators fearing that Julius' reckless use of power would be detrimental for them, will assassinate him.

20. Then Augustus Caesar, the great-nephew of Julius Caesar, will become Emperor of Rome. He will be known for imposing a great census upon the whole empire. However, a few years after this census is imposed, he will die. But, his death will not be in a murderous rage like his great-uncle. Instead, Augustus will die at an old age of natural causes.

21. The next Emperor who obtains the Roman throne will be Tiberius Caesar. Tiberius will have a dark, reclusive personality and will later be known as the gloomiest man on earth. He will also obtain a bad reputation and will not be given the honor of a Caesar. In all actuality, the only reason Tiberius comes into the prosperity of the throne is through adoption, which will be manipulated by his mother through her marriage to Augustus.

22. Several years later, the Jews will seal their fate. The armies of Rome will overwhelm Jerusalem like a flood, destroying the city, the temple, and scattering its inhabitants. Understand that Jerusalem's desolation is a direct result of the Jew's rejection of the Messiah. Their rejection of Christ will lead Him to be crucified

on the cross.

23. Centuries later, Rome will begin experiencing an influx of Barbarian tribes invading from the north. The Vandal tribe, led by King Genseric, will sign a peace treaty with the Roman Empire; but this will turn out to be a big deception as the Vandals will break the treaty and continue attacking Rome. The Vandals will grow into a strong, powerful nation, even though they'll begin as a small insignificant tribe.

24. The Vandals will come into prosperity by taking the rich grain-producing lands of North Africa. King Genseric will also do something that none of his ancestors ever accomplished—he will take the wealth of Africa and distribute it amongst his people. The Vandals will also devise various schemes to raid and pillage other essential regions within the empire.

25. Recognized by Rome as the new King of the South, the Vandals will continue to loot and plunder the Roman Empire. The destruction caused by the Barbarians will provoke Rome's emperors to send one of the largest armies ever assembled to destroy the Vandals once and for all. However, the Vandals will also rally their army to neutralize the threat posed by the Roman army. At the conclusion of this war, known as the Battle of Cape Bon, half of the Roman fleet will be destroyed, and thousands of Roman soldiers will be killed. Rome will ultimately lose this war because of the tactics employed by the Vandals.

26. You see, King Genseric will bribe top Roman officials to provide the Vandals with key military intelligence. He will even convince multiple Roman Navy captains to switch allegiances to him along with their ships. This is how the Vandals will often overwhelm Rome's armies and is also why Rome will lose many soldiers to them in battle.

27. Years later, Genseric's grandson, Hilderic, will be the king of the Vandals. However, Hilderic will plot to stop his cousin, Gelimer from succeeding him, and Gelimer will conspire to take the throne away from Hilderic. Both the current king and the king-in-waiting will sit at the same royal table and pretend they are not plotting against one other. Unfortunately for them, neither king's plan will succeed as the Vandal's allotted time as the King of the South is about to come to an end.

28. Around this time, an emperor named Justinian I will inherit the Roman throne. However, after nearly bankrupting the kingdom, he'll begin confiscating his citizen's wealth in order to restore the nation's treasury. He will also declare the Bishop of Rome to be the head of all church affairs, which will eventually become an attack against the New Covenant. However, before all this happens, Justinian will have his heart set on retaking all the lands that were previously conquered by the Barbarian tribes. Justinian will begin this re-conquest campaign

against the Vandals.

29. Remember, God has already determined when the Vandalic Kingdom will end. Therefore, at that designated time, the Roman armies will return to the south to destroy the Vandals. But this time, the war will not end in Rome's defeat as it did in the Battle of Cartagena, and the Battle of Cape Bon.

30. At that time, the Vandal fleet will be moving against Sardinia to neutralize the revolt. This diversion will allow Roman forces to bypass the Vandal fleet and engage the Vandal forces on land. At the conclusion of this conflict, known as the Vandalic War, the Vandals will be destroyed, and North Africa will be restored to the Roman Empire. However, around this same time, Emperor Justinian will also become more involved in matters of the Church and will begin enacting laws that defy God's holy covenant. Even though Justinian will be known for recovering a large portion of Roman territory, he will also be known as the one who will conspire with the Bishop of Rome to elevate him as the head of the Church.

31. Once the Bishop of Rome is declared to be the head of Christianity, the Papacy will be established. Armies will enforce its policies; it will regain its seat of authority over the sanctuary in Rome; and Christianity, which is the continuation of Judaism, will be taken away and replaced by Catholicism, the Pagan-Christian mixture that results in ruin.

32. Emperor Justinian will corrupt many by rewarding all who convert to this religion. However, many will see through the Papacy's lies and preserve the knowledge of the truth, and God will strengthen them.

33. These individuals will expose Catholicism by teaching the truth from God's Word. Unfortunately, they and their followers will be persecuted for their faith. Many of them will be killed by the sword, some of them will be burned alive, and others will be held captive as if they are the spoils of war. This will continue for over a thousand years.

34. Even though many will die during this period of persecution, God will help them by raising up a reformer named Martin Luther. This theologian will challenge the actions of the Catholic Church, giving birth to a movement known as the Protestant Reformation. Though some of the princes will support this movement, many of them will be persuaded to continue clinging to Papal beliefs.

35. Those who follow Martin Luther's protest will be known as Protestant Christians. Many of these Protestants will fall. They will be placed on trial and executed, but they will also be made spotless in the eyes of God—especially during the 1260 years of persecution, which will end at the time it was prophesied.

36. However, prior to its downfall, the Papacy will do

whatever it wants. It will exalt and magnify itself as if it were Jehovah, thereby exalting itself above every other god. The Papacy will make blasphemous statements and laws against the God of gods and shall prosper until it is overthrown in 1798 AD. The Papacy's fall has already been determined by God and will happen exactly when He says it will.

37. But you should also know that during the Papacy's reign, another power will emerge. Turkish Muslims will rise and consolidate into a nation known as the Ottoman Empire. Even though their ancestors will be Christian, the Ottomans will have no regard for the God whom their fathers worshipped. They'll also have no regard for the veneration of Mary, the desired woman. In fact, they won't force those who they conquer to recognize any particular god as their priority will be on military conquests.

38. But, in their territories, they will give preference to Allah—the god of Mecca. Though entirely unknown to their ancestors, the Ottomans will honor this deity in their mosques and temples decorated with gold, silver, and expensive ornaments.

39. The honor given to this foreign deity will be clearly acknowledged in Ottoman-controlled territories as it increases in glory and influence among the nations. The Ottoman Empire will expand and rule over many, but in the end, their Empire will fall and be partitioned to benefit other countries.

40. However, several years later, Islamic militants from the King of the South's territory will launch a terrorist attack against the King of the North—the United States of America. This assault, known as the 911 Terror Attacks, will result in airplanes crashing, skyscrapers crumbling, and thousands of people losing their lives. The United States of America will respond to this attack by launching a War on Terror. US forces will destroy multiple terrorist targets like a category five hurricane with tanks, Humvees, and many warships. America will attack many of the Middle Eastern countries by toppling regimes and setting up new ones.

41. Years after the War on Terror subsides, Islamic countries will launch a major attack against Jerusalem. This attack will prompt the United States to send its troops into this region of Palestine in order to defend Israel from its enemies. The United States and its allies will overthrow multiple countries in the Middle East, but Jordan will escape the onslaught as America will honor God's original command to spare them.

42. Egypt, however, will not escape. The United States and its allies will topple this regime along with others.

43. America will establish financial control over Egypt's wealth and its economy. However, Egypt will not be alone in its submission to the superpower. Libya and Sudan will also be forced to follow Egypt's footsteps

and be under the control of the United States and its allies.
44. While all of this is happening, rumors of war will sound from Turkey and the Middle East. This threat will alarm America to the point that they will focus their war efforts against the whole Middle Eastern region. This war will be fought with great fury, and many will die as a result.
45. At the conclusion of this war, the Papacy will emerge as a universal peace-keeping broker. The United States will then establish the Papacy's headquarters in Israel between the Mediterranean and Dead seas in order to prepare the world to receive Satan when he personates Jesus in Jerusalem. In the end, those who follow the lies of the Papacy and False Protestant Christianity will be destroyed along with Satan, and no one will be able to save them.

Daniel 12

Three Prophetic Periods

1. While the world is in a state of turmoil, Michael, the Great Prince, and defender of Israel, will finish His work as our High Priest in the heavenly sanctuary, and then He will stand up. At the moment He stands, the world will begin experiencing a time of trouble that will produce more devastation than any nation has previously caused. But God will save your people—those whose names are written in the Book of Life.

2. However, many of them, whose names are written in the Book of Life, will already be dead. So when Michael comes back to this earth, He will resurrect them from their graves. Most of the resurrected will be raised to receive everlasting life; however, those who had an active part in His crucifixion will also be resurrected to see Him sitting on the right hand of Power. They will see the Son for who He is, and they will experience shame and everlasting contempt for what they did.

3. But those who know and teach the Word of God will reflect the light that exudes from Christ at His Second Coming. They will shine like a bright afternoon sky, and those who helped win souls to Christ shall glow like heaven's stars on a clear night. Their reward will last forever.

4. But Daniel, I want you to understand that the full explanation of these visions will be hidden and concealed until the time of the end, which will begin after the fall of the Papacy. During that time, many

will become inspired to search for the meaning of these prophecies, and God will begin raising up men and women with the knowledge to understand them."

5. After this, the scene changed, and I saw two angels standing by the banks of a river. One angel stood on the river bank closest to me, and the other angel stood on the river bank that was on the other side.

6. Then, one of the angels asked Jesus, who was wearing linen garments and hovering over the river, "How long will it be until the end, when your power is manifested, and people begin to understand these prophecies?"

7. Then I watched the Son of God, who was dressed in linen and hovering over the water. As He lifted both of His hands towards heaven, I listened as He swore by God the Father, who is immortal, and told me that these things would be allowed to continue for 1260 years, and then He will put an end to the hand that's crushing the holy people. This is when the persecution of the dark ages will be finished.

8. I heard what He said, but I couldn't understand how 1260 years correlated to the restoration of the sanctuary. So then I said, "My Lord, how will all of this end?"

9. He responded and said, "This is as much as I am going to tell you, Daniel, because the meaning of this vision is hidden and concealed from understanding

until the end of the 1260 years.

10. Until then, many will be persecuted, and attempts will be made to wipe the true believers off the face of this earth. Yes, the wicked will continue to do wicked things, but they won't understand what I've shown you. Only the wise will know the truth.

11. However, please know that when the time comes for Christianity, which is the continuation of Judaism, to be taken away and replaced by Catholicism, the Pagan-Christian mixture, 1290 years will have passed from the time of Rome's founding.

12. Even though God's people will be persecuted, He will ultimately vindicate them in the judgment. Therefore whoever faithfully waits and yearns for God to cleanse His sanctuary will be blessed when their name comes up in the judgment. This judgment will begin 1305 years after Catholicism replaces the Christian Church.

13. So go about the rest of your life until the time comes for you to rest in the grave. But be assured, at the appointed time, the prophecies you recorded will speak to those who will be alive during the time of the end.

THE CLEAR AND PRESENT TRUTH OF
DANIEL

www.ingramcontent.com/pod-product-compliance
Lightning Source LLC
Chambersburg PA
CBHW070939080526
44589CB00013B/1578